POCKET GUIDE TO THE VOICE

WRITTEN BY RUTH ROYALL

Pocket Guide to the Voice

First published 2019

Paperback ISBN: 978 1 78645 341 9
eBook ISBN: 978 1 78645 350 1

Design: Ruth Royall

Proofreading, typesetting and formatting:
Beaten Track Publishing,
Burscough, Lancashire.
www.beatentrackpublishing.com

Just to Say Thank You...

I want to say a big thank-you to my family for supporting me every step of the way. Special thanks to Mamma Royall for her beautiful illustrations of the body and also to Uncle Geoff for bringing Ellie to life.

Thank you to my partner Sam for believing in me and giving me the time and space to bring this idea to life. Your patience and belief has been paramount.

Thank you to my mentors Gillyanne Kayes and Jeremy Fisher of Vocal Process. Your support, knowledge and belief in what I do is invaluable.

And finally, thank you to my friends. Thank you for fiercely supporting me in everything I do.

Welcome to the Pocket Guide to the Voice

Let me introduce myself. My name is Ruth Royall. I'm a vocalist, songwriter and vocal coach.

I do all kinds of things. I've toured with some pretty cool bands, I've sung on the telly (you might even have heard me!), I've written music for a fair few people, and I've released some music of my own.

I've also spent the last eight years learning about how the voice works. I'm a self-proclaimed voice nerd, and I love helping other people discover their own amazing vocal instrument.

Since I started teaching, I've learned that people learn best when taught habits.

Learning to sing doesn't mean you'll be able to sing Whitney by the end of lesson one. However, by using healthy habits, we can create a solid foundation to the voice in no time at all!

Just remember: the voice is part of our body, and the more we use our body the healthier and stronger it gets.

This book is a collection of exercises and methods that allows you to navigate your way through the voice and pick up some useful information on the way.

That's really what this book is all about...

Contents

Who Should Use This Book?

Anyone! This book is perfect if you're just starting out and you've never sung a note in your life. It's also great if you want to dip in and refresh your memory. It can be used again and again as all the exercises in the book are part of a healthy vocal diet. I've tried out a lot of these exercises on some of the more advanced vocalists I teach, and they work a treat! New or experienced, old or young, this book can be consumed by all!

What This Book Won't Do:

This book won't teach you to sing like Mariah Carey (only Mariah can do that). It won't teach you to master that top Eb and get you belting like Freddie Mercury at the top of your lungs. This book is about building steady and reliable vocal practice through simple and consistent exercises.

What This Book Will Do:

This book WILL give you a clear understanding of how your voice works. It will help you to build a solid foundation that you can then take on to use as you wish. It will teach you HEALTHY habits and do so in an easy, manageable and fun way. Sound good? Then let's get started!

What is an Elephant Burger?

How do you eat an elephant? No, really! Desmond Tutu once said wisely that 'there is only one way to eat an elephant: a bite at a time', and he was right!

Just like learning to sing, you can't do it all at once. So we do it one bite at a time or, as I like to say, in elephant burgers!

We are going to eat one elephant burger a day until we have eaten the whole elephant (sorry, vegans, I hope you understand this is a metaphor, and no elephants were harmed in the making of this book). This is Ellie who will help us on our journey through the voice.

Hi, Ellie! By doing it this way, we will build up a solid, physical foundation for the voice and we won't forget! (I mean, elephants never forget, right?)

Being consistent with your vocal practice and not rushing will embed these skills into your body. Our brain processes learning in four stages:

1. Unconscious incompetence – this means you are doing something wrong but you don't realise.
2. Conscious incompetence – this means that you are doing something wrong but you are aware of it.
3. Conscious competence – this is where you are doing something right but you need to think about it, and finally...

4. Unconscious competence – this is where you are doing something right but you don't notice. A great example of this is riding a bike. Most people do this without even thinking, but your body had to learn at some point!

How to Use This Book:

This book is a pocket guide, which means you can literally carry it around in your pocket and dip into it as and when it pleases you. You should spend at least a day with each exercise. They are written in such a way that you can incorporate them into your daily routine – nifty! Keep it fun, don't pressure yourself to do an hour's practice a day standing in front of the mirror. That comes later. For now, it's just about getting to grips with the basics. This book can be finished as quickly or a slowly as you choose. You can eat it all in one sitting, or you can consume it gradually and savour every mouthful.

The book is split into four categories:

1. Body
2. Breath
3. Mechanism
4. Resonance

They won't necessarily go in that order. However, you will notice that the tasks gradually get more in depth as the book goes on, and it's useful to know which part of the voice you're working on.

Body

This one pretty much does what it says on the tin. These elephant burgers will focus on our body, posture and balance. The voice is like a clock and we need to focus on much more than just where the sound is created. If our posture isn't right, it affects the sound we make. If we don't stretch properly, it makes it harder for us to produce those sweet, sweet melodies.

Think of your body as the foundation and frame to your voice. You need to create a sturdy yet flexible structure to allow your voice to work properly. If you carry a lot of tension in your body, you may find it hard to control the voice or reach certain notes.

Breath

These elephant burgers will focus on the respiratory system and breath technique. A lot of these exercises can be incorporated into your day-to-day life to bring a little peace and quiet. Bliss!

Remember: breath plays a big part in actually producing sound in the first place. It's our power! Without enough breath, the vocal folds will find it hard to properly oscillate, meaning the sound produced can feel weak and you may easily run out of breath altogether. Getting your breath functioning like a well-oiled machine will stand you in good stead. Understanding how the respiratory system works will mean you can keep a good air flow going and sing to your heart's content!

Mechanism

These elephant burgers will focus on our mechanism. Our mechanism is the parts of our body that actually create the sound, for example: your larynx and your vocal folds. These are super tiny but vital! We can manipulate these parts of our body to create the sound and texture we want. Amazing!

Your larynx is a little delicate; you'll naturally feel you don't want to poke or prod around too vigorously in these areas. It is a fragile and incredible small piece of machinery and we must take care of it. Warm-ups and warm-downs are a must in keeping your larynx happy. This guide will give you some handy tips on how to keep your mechanism in tip-top condition.

Resonance

The definition of resonance means sound reflecting off a surface or object. In the voice, this is how we create tone. We can also use resonance to help us increase volume. The human voice is amazing!

We are basically big reed instruments. Instead of a reed we have vocal folds, but unlike reed instruments we can change our resonating space. An oboe will only ever sound like an oboe. We can sound like a barking dog or a crying baby by changing the space that the sound bounces off. Neat!

In this guide, we'll explore how we can manipulate our resonance and how to increase the volume of our voice without straining that precious voice.

How to Build a Habit:

We build habits by creating a loop. This loop consists of cue – routine – reward. We have lots of these loops in our daily lives such as: walk into bathroom (cue) – clean teeth (routine) – teeth feel smooth and clean (reward). A reward as small as this is enough to build a habit. By creating a regular routine that consists of these loops, we can consciously build habits. This relates to singing because our voice is a muscle; the more we use it, the stronger it gets. If we consistently build these healthy habits, we will see a dramatic improvement in our voices.

Here is an example: Arrive at choir practice (cue) – do a vocal warm-up and stretch (routine) – have a sip of your favourite herbal tea that you brought with you (reward). Just that one sip is enough to create that brain loop.

Here's another: Step up to a microphone (cue) – align your posture (routine) – feel balanced and relaxed (reward).

Smells, emotions, even small physical feelings are enough to create a habit. Being conscious of this is very powerful as we can choose what habits we want to build. The buzz of endorphins you get after a session at the gym is enough to build a habit; your job is to be consistent at repeating that habit enough times for the body to take over and do it without thinking.

Studies show you need to repeat a routine 21 times before it becomes a habit. Easy-peasy! Before you know it, you'll be warming up without even thinking about it because it's become a habit.

⭐ What is a Nugget?

Calling all vocal nerds! This is the science-y bit. Little nuggets will appear throughout this book to provide you with information about anatomy and the functions of the voice. They are super easy to digest and all very interesting so I highly recommend you stay tuned!

💪 What is a Challenge?

We all love a challenge, right? You'll find fun little tasks and challenges dotted throughout this guide. Don't feel like you have to do them, but I promise you it will be jolly fun if you do!

It's All in the Hips!

So here goes! Our first elephant burger.

It doesn't just apply to salsa dancers when they say it's all in the hips! Our hips/pelvic area is our centre of balance. When we align this correctly, it helps the rest of our body balance out. Our spine is shaped like an S, and it's important to know that we're not looking to straighten it out. Oh no! We're looking for balance. This means that you need to stay flexible. Once you've found your balance, make sure you keep a little movement in the body.

Walking around the room or going from a sitting position to standing is great to help find your balance. The main thing is to stay conscious of how your body feels, right down to your toes.

Elephant Burger:

Either sitting or standing, we are going to engage our centre of balance. Imagine you are doing your flies up. As you do so, engage your pelvic muscle so your bottom tucks underneath you. It's important to note here that not everyone needs to actually 'tip' their hips; this exercise is more about locating and engaging your centre of balance to give you a good amount of support.

As you engage your pelvic muscle, notice what happens to your back. You should feel a change in posture. If you are standing, notice what happens to your knees. They should soften slightly. Keep checking in with yourself and moving your hips from side to side as well as forward and back to make sure you are flexible and comfortable.

It's important not to tip your hips too far forward, as this can feel a little uncomfortable. Our bodies usually have a position that they are used to being in. Women often arch their backs, this is natural, but too much can cause discomfort at the base of the back. Men often stand with their feet further apart. Again, this is normal but can sometimes make their shoulders hunch over, which can cause discomfort.

Make sure you are aware of these things and listen to your body. It's very clever and will know when it's

in the right place. Keep doing this hip-tuck exercise through the day – you may even feel a little taller by the end of it! Remember: you can do it sitting or standing.

Top Tip: If you feel yourself stiffening up at any point or you feel a little uncomfortable, just give yourself a little wiggle. This will release any tension and keep you flexible.

Stretch!

Everyone loves a good stretch in the morning. I personally think a cat would be my spirit animal. Not only do I love a good stretch, but I jump at the opportunity to sun myself in a window.

Stretching is super good for the voice. It helps to release any tension in our muscles and gets us physically aware of our bodies. It's sometimes easy to forget about this incredible piece of machinery we walk around in everyday, when we are surrounded by distractions all the time. Singing is a physical activity, and it's important that we spend some time getting in tune with our physical selves.

Here is a list of some stretches that are great for the voice. Try to incorporate them into your morning routine (I promise, they feel gooooooood).

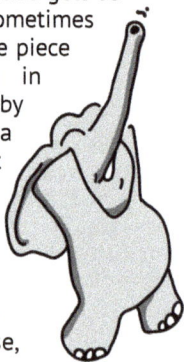

Elephant Burger:

- From a standing position, let your head drop forward and roll down slowly, keeping your head loose like a bell and your arms swinging in front of you. Once you've rolled all the way down, as far as is comfortable, slowly bring yourself back up, keeping your head loose so you can feel the stretch right down your back. Remember to keep your knees soft.
- Lace your fingers together in front of you, push your palms away from you and lift them above your head.
- Push one shoulder at a time up towards the sky. You should feel a deep stretch into your back.
- Shoulder rolls.
- Shoulder lifts: lift your shoulders up to your ears and then let them flop down again.
- Look down. *(Stretch the back of the neck.)*
- Lift your chin up, placing your hands at the base of your neck at the front. *(Stretch the front of your neck.)*
- Roll your head to either side and hold.
- Chewing and face stretches.

Do as many as you can. Even just doing a few face stretches while you clean your teeth in the morning is all good stuff. Also it looks hilarious in the mirror. Better still, make it a habit. Remember the system! Cue – maybe when your alarm goes or after you clean your teeth. Routine – stretch. Reward!! – treat yourself with your morning coffee once your stretches are complete!

Tummy Flop

You heard me! Today is all about letting that belly hang out. This is our first breath exercise and is hilarious fun. We are going to work from the out-breath first. This is a really good thing to get into; it sets us up really well and means we don't over-breathe and take in too much air.

Elephant Burger:

Place your hands on your tummy with your thumb placed over your belly button. Exhale in a long breath, 'psshh', with the same pressure you would use to blow out a candle. As you do this, you will feel your belly button moving back towards your spine. Exhale until there is nothing left. (Remember: you don't need to take a breath in to do this; use the air that is already in the your lungs.) You will feel your tummy muscles working to hold this position in place once your lungs are empty. Then simply let that tension go and let your belly flop out. (Don't be shy!) As you do this movement, your diaphragm will contract, allowing your lungs to fill with air again. It's important that you let the air 'drop in' and you don't try to pull in a long, slow breath. Your lungs will fill up quickly and naturally.

It's important to let your tummy muscles go completely floppy when you do this. It's soooooo tempting to hold your tummy in and try to control the in-breath.

12

But you must persist! Floppy tummy = happy breath! And the great thing is, you can do this wherever you are! When you're in the shower, when you're walking the dog, pretending to listen intently to your neighbour about his veg patch, when really you're doing the belly flop exercise... ;)

💪 Challenge!

Why not give mindfulness a go? Mindfulness is all about the breath and being in the moment. There are some super cool apps out there you can use (I recommend Headspace). You only have to do it for two minutes if you struggle sitting still. While you sit and feel peaceful, use your new belly-flop exercise and simply count the breaths. Bliss!

Controlled breathing is an excellent way to manage stress. Controlled breathing triggers something called our 'parasympathetic nervous system' (*whaaat?*). This is linked to the stimulation of the vagus nerve. The vagus nerve is a nerve that runs from the base of the brain to the abdomen and is responsible for mediating nervous system responses and lowering heart rate.

So basically, in a nutshell, controlled breathing calms us, steadies our blood flow and makes us feel all warm and fuzzy.

⭐ Nugget!

The diaphragm is shaped like a large parachute. It's attached to the base of your lungs and sits above your stomach and intestines. The diaphragm works by contracting and relaxing as we inhale and exhale. As the diaphragm contracts, it pulls the lungs open, causing you to suck in and fill your lungs with air.

The best thing about this is it works without you even trying! Notice how we don't die in our sleep and stuff? Well, that's because our body instinctively makes sure our diaphragm is working all the time, to keep us breathing and alive!

Check out the diagram below. The image on the left is the diaphragm contracting and pulling the air in. The one on the right is the diaphragm relaxing and letting the air out.

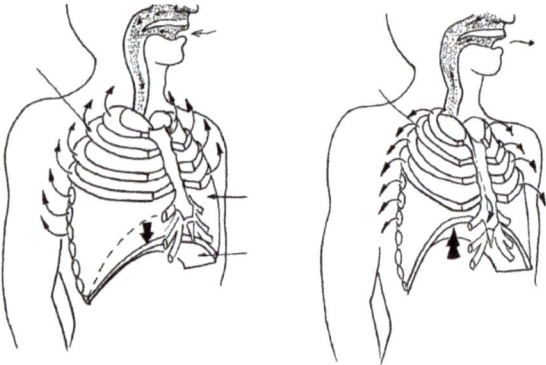

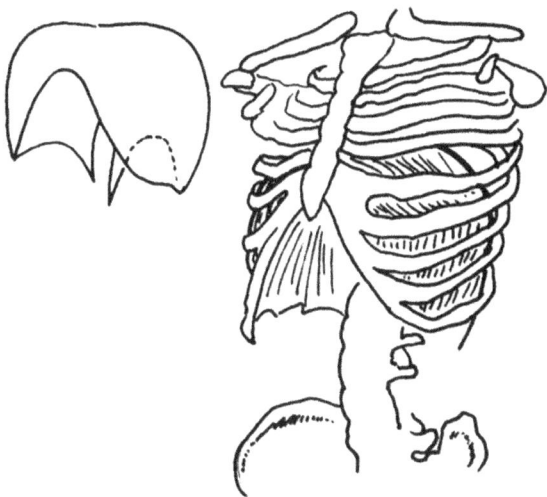

THE DIAPHRAGM

This diagram is great as it shows you how big the diaphragm is and its actual shape.

You can see that the diaphragm sits inside your ribcage and goes quite far down your back.

This means you should be able to feel your breath expanding all the way around your body.

Warm-Ups!

I always stretch as part of my warm-up and I suggest you include a good stretch as part of yours. It is also important to include some voiced warm-ups as part of your warm-up too. The voice needs to get moving before you start singing properly. You'd never see a runner or a gymnast start without a warm-up! Well, we must think of the voice in the same way. It needs to be warm so it doesn't get damaged or strained. A warm voice will mean more flexibility and a better tone overall.

Elephant Burger:

Warm-ups don't need to take all day as long as you do the right ones. We are going to focus on soft, safe sounds. Make sure you are breathing properly as this will really help your warm-ups. Placing your thumbs in your belly button and your hands pointing down to form a diamond shape, give a couple of short soft 'mm-hm's as if you are softly agreeing with someone. Do this a few times (you'll be able to feel the muscles contracting under your fingers).

Now, imagine you are about to eat something super yummy; lengthen the sound into a slow siren starting from a high note and ending up nice and low. Remember to keep those sounds soft and gentle; if your voice doesn't come out, don't push it! Let it do its thing. After you've done this a few times, progress into fricatives. Fricatives are buzzy sounds such as 'vvvv' and 'zzzz'. We're going to work with 'vvvv':

make a gentle revving sound as if you are revving a motorbike engine. Try three in a row. It's important to allow your tummy to move in and out (you can monitor this with your hands). Try the revs on each breath. Allow your voice to siren up and down to where feels comfortable. Try some different sounds like 'zzzz' and 'jjjj'. Going from high to low is great for the voice and really helps to loosen everything up.

Now try some lip rolls. Doing the same sirens, bring your lips together in a 'brrrrr' sound as if you were impersonating a helicopter. Some people find it easier to put their fingers either side of their mouth and push up slightly to help with the lip-roll, but only do this if you are struggling with the warm-up.

Allow the voice to slide around in gentle sirens. It's important to try and slow the sirens down so you are singing all the notes in the siren and not skipping lots.

You only need to spend 5-10 minutes on your vocalised warm-ups as long as you've stretched properly. You'll notice your voice behaves differently at different times of day. Most singers have an optimum time of day they like to sing as they feel this is when their voice is the most 'open'. See if you can spot when your voice feels the most flexible.

Diamonds Are Forever

This exercise is called The Support Diamond. I first discovered this exercise when I read Gillyanne Kayes' *Singing and The Actor*. She also credited Janice Chapman and Meribeth Dayme for their research and work on the subject. I find this exercise really helpful in showing you where your support comes from. It's all about having a balance of happy tension in the body.

Elephant Burger:

Place your hands on your waist just under your ribcage (the squishy bit). Give a short, sharp 'puh'. You should feel something pushing against your hands as you make this sound. Now bring two fingers to the dip in you ribcage at the front of your torso and two fingers to the top of your pubic bone above your groin area. Again, give a short, sharp 'puh'. You should feel this same pushing against your fingers. If you can't feel much movement at these points, try readjusting your posture. Your balance and posture can really affect your support diamond.

Another thing you'll notice is the muscles in your torso contracting as you exhale. Notice how they are moving. The muscles will feel like they are contracting up from your groin area. Your tummy should remain squishy to allow

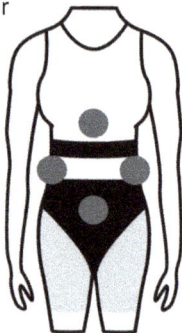

the breath easily in and out. This diamond shape gives us a great frame and support for our breath, and it also helps to show us if our posture is balanced or not. The tension that you are feeling as you exhale is coming from quite low down. There is an 'up and under' sensation going on. Once you've got the hang of this movement, remember to give yourself a little wiggle. When we concentrate too hard, the body sometimes stiffens up. Give yourself a little wiggle to reset.

Toffee Teeth

OK, so sadly this exercise doesn't involve toffee. The mind is a powerful thing! If we imagine it hard enough, maybe we'll actually believe we have toffee in our teeth...

This exercise is all about the tongue. The tongue is mahoosive! It fills almost our entire mouth and jaw. I didn't include our tongue in the stretching elephant burger. As it's so cool, I felt it deserved its very own elephant burger.

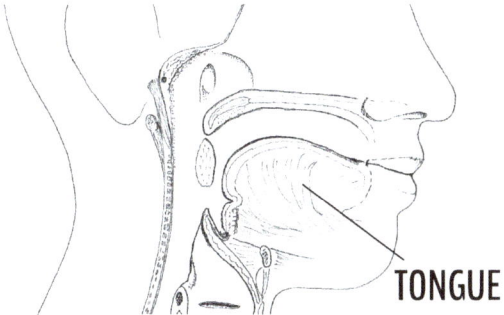

TONGUE

Elephant Burger:

First of all, imagine you have toffee stuck in your teeth. Reach your tongue to the back bottom tooth on the right-hand side and hold for five seconds; now do the same on the left and hold for five; now the top right and hold for five; now the top left and hold for five.

Now make circles in your right cheek five times one way and five times the other, then do the same in your left cheek. Now roll the tongue around the inside of the front of your mouth, behind your lips. Do this five times one way and five times the other. Now stick your tongue out as far as possible and hold for five. Do this three times. Make sure all the movements are slow – you should really start to feel it by the end!! You can do this once a day or you can do it more! Have fun with it!

Challenge!

Do it in public! No doubt you look hilarious when you do this stretch, so let go of any fear and stretch that tongue at the gym! If anyone asks what you are doing, you can say you're eating elephant burgers. ;)

Find Your Feet

Look down…there they are! All right, you got me, that isn't the whole exercise. This elephant burger is all about balance. We have three points on our feet that create a triangle. A triangle is a very sturdy shape and creates an excellent structure for our body. There are also arches on your feet that should be slightly lifted. Check the diagram below to see where these are.

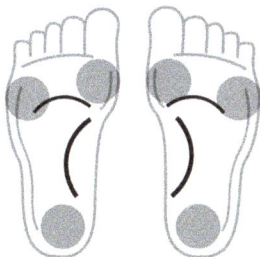

Elephant Burger:

Align your balance *(Top Tip: use your hips!)* and roll the weight around your feet. Find the three points and make sure your arches are slightly lifted. Be sure not to scrunch up your toes; your toes are very important, and make sure we don't fall over (although that would be very funny for anyone watching). Simply take a few steps feeling the structure in your feet. Does it change how you feel? Does it change your posture at all? Spend the day finding your feet and getting nice and grounded.

Tummy Dance

Do the tummy daaaaance! Today, we are going to be getting those tummy muscles working. This elephant burger will really support your tummy-flop exercise. Awareness is key. Make sure you notice what is happening as you do it. Adjust your posture, find your feet and get that tummy dancing!

Elephant Burger:

Using your tummy muscles, pull your tummy in as if you're posing in front of the mirror to take a selfie (don't pretend you don't!) then let that tummy flop out. As you pull your tummy in, check what you can feel engaging. You should be able to feel your obliques working as you pull your tummy in – you can check out where the obliques are in the nugget below. When you release your tummy, your rectus abdominus (aka your six-pack, grrr...) should act like a sling to catch your tummy. Make sure you are totally letting this muscle go and not holding any tension in your upper abs. You can also try doing this as you breathe, as long as you've made sure your tummy has learnt all the dance moves.

Your obliques should act like a pulley system, pulling your tummy up and in. Try not to focus on your abdominals when pulling your tummy in; focus on the obliques. You can use the diamond support exercise to help you here as well.

⭐ Nugget!

I'm not going to go too crazy with muscle names here as there are loads and they are hard to spell. The most important thing is to know where the main muscle groups are and how it should feel when you are standing correctly.

It's helpful to know that all the muscles in the body pull; nothing pushes. We are like a big, very intricate pulley system. This means that when we are moving in two different directions (for example, tipping our hips forwards and backwards) we are using two different sets of muscles to create this movement.

Some of the main muscles we engage to create a balanced posture are the EXTERNAL OBLIQUES, INTERNAL OBLIQUES, TRANSVERSUS ABDOMINIS and our RECTUS ABDOMINIS – all together called our abs. Grrr...

We engage these muscles when we tip our hips forward to create our 'soft knee' position and also use them when we are exhaling our breath.

You can check out some diagrams of these muscles on the next page. Try having a little feel around as well and see if you can feel them contract and release.

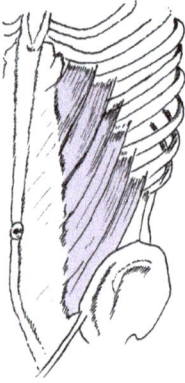

EXTERNAL OBLIQUES

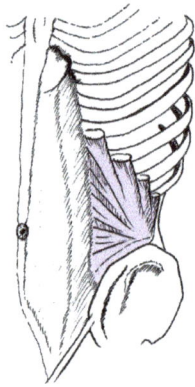

INTERNAL OBLIQUES

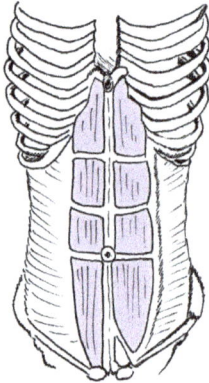

INTERNAL OBLIQUES

The Out-Breath

Starting on the out breath is a wondrous thing. It sets us up for the inhale and means we don't over breathe. It's very tempting when we start from the in breath, to suck in as much air as possible, to lift our shoulders and create some uncomfortable tension in our throat.

Interesting Fact: When we quickly pull air into the upper part of our lungs creating a shallow 'gasp' sensation, it triggers our body into the 'fight or flight' response, which has evolved as a survival mechanism. Our body floods with adrenaline and our heart rate increases to help us run away from oncoming bears! Great! Unless there are no bears... Low breathing or 'diaphragmatic breathing', where we pull our diaphragm right down and let our lungs fill up naturally, means that we don't trigger this reaction. Phew!

Elephant Burger:

Today, we are going to focus on realigning ourselves with our out-breath. This is great as it helps us practise our tummy dance and also our tummy flop! But this time we are concentrating on how it feels to exhale! Work those obliques and make sure your posture is balanced. Throughout the day, take a minute to exhale before you start doing anything. Before you get in the shower, exhale. Before you get in your car, exhale. Before you walk into your first meeting, exhale. Notice how it sets your body up. A nice bonus is that it will also calm you down and clear your head a little. Nifty!

⭐ Nugget!

As you know, every muscle in the body pulls; nothing pushes. They pull in the direction that the muscle fibres are going. This is why we have so many layers of muscles, and why they are all angled in different directions. I like to think of it like this: imagine there are little people with ropes either side of your body.

When you lean backwards, the ropes are pulling on your back; this is what makes you tip backwards. In order for you to not tip completely backwards and fall over, the ropes at the front of your body are also working but not pulling as hard. This ensures that you don't fall over!

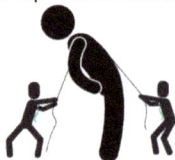

Another word for this is 'engaged'. This means that the muscle is working but not hard enough to pull you in that direction, just enough to support you. We use this 'engaged' level of muscle tension a lot in singing.

Body-Balance Breath

This exercise does require some equipment. Exercise balls are great for this, or you can use something called a balance trainer. If you don't have these, but you are a member of a gym, they will definitely have some version of either or both. Another (slightly uncomfortable) alternative to this is a basketball. If you can get hold of a slightly deflated basketball then that would be a little more comfortable on the bottom!

Elephant Burger:

Sit yourself comfortably on your exercise ball. Roll yourself around a little and notice which muscles engage to keep you upright. You'll feel a little comfortable tension or 'happy tension' in your pelvic muscles, your back and your abdominals. This creates a really good core structure to your torso. Once you've found your balance, start to add in your belly-flop breath exercise. Notice how it feels. Has anything changed? Do you feel more or less tension?

⭐ Nugget!

What is happy tension? Tension isn't always a bad thing. We need some level of tension in our body to keep us from flopping all over the place. What we need to make sure is that we don't transfer the tension to parts of the body that can't cope with it. Our big muscle groups such as our abs, our lats (back muscles) and our legs are great for holding happy tension and keeping a good level of support in our body. We can still create unhappy tension in these areas. If we start squeezing our muscles, we know that we have surpassed happy tension and ventured into the realms of constriction. Using an exercise ball helps to show your body what level of tension you want in the body.

💪 Challenge!

Try swapping your office chair for either a balance trainer or an exercise ball. It will work wonders if you are experiencing any back pain and will help your overall posture immensely!

Like I said before, we spend a huge amount of time sitting down and hunching over laptops. This can cause quite a lot of discomfort. Simply having a little more awareness of your body can help. Stretching regularly and using something like a balance trainer or exercise ball keeps your body flexible and keeps the support muscles in use.

It's always good to take breaks. Look out the window ever hour or so, take a little walk around the room or to the kettle to break up the day. While you're there, you can practise some posture and belly-flop exercises too!

Feel the Buzz

So where is the sound actually coming from? That would be your larynx! Ah yes, that tiny, beautifully designed piece of machinery we call the larynx. It's an amazing piece of equipment, and we all have one! This elephant burger will be spent locating yours. It's important to remember that everyone's is different. Some people find it really easy to locate theirs, some people struggle. Don't worry! Just be gentle with yourself and have a little poke around until you can feel something.

It is worth mentioning, you will want to be gentle when you are feeling around for your larynx. It is a delicate thing and you will naturally want to be careful.

Elephant Burger:

Place your hand over your throat and take a good swallow. Feel something lifting and dropping? That's your larynx! Guys will find this easier than ladies as theirs are bigger. The front of the larynx is also called the 'Adam's apple' and protrudes a little more on men than it does on women. Once you've located that little bump place your hand in front of your mouth and sigh. You'll feel the air travelling up into your mouth and hitting your hand, but you won't feel anything happening in your larynx. This is because your vocal folds have not come together yet so nothing is vibrating. Now try a gentle 'AH' sound. Whoa!!! Loads of buzzing! That's your larynx! Now you've started to create a sound, your vocal folds have come together and started to vibrate and you can really feel it! Spend the day thinking about your larynx. What is it doing? How does it move when you speak? If you feel any tension in it, just swallow and take a breath and this will bring it back to a nice relaxed neutral position.

⭐ Nugget!

Let's meet the larynx! The larynx is a tiny pulley system that works with our vocal tract to create sound. It's important to have an idea of how the larynx fits together as being able to visualise the larynx will help you manipulate it.

The larynx is a collection of cartilage, muscle and one bone, the hyoid bone (woo!). The larynx houses the vocal folds and is positioned at the top of the TRACHEA (the windpipe).

Its main function is to help us go between breathing and swallowing. It protects our lungs from any bits of food that might venture in there and make us choke. When we close the larynx and stop breathing, it helps us push. We need to do this when we give birth (puuuuuush!), when we vomit and, um...other bodily functions such as... *cough*...poo!

The larynx manoeuvres our vocal folds, allowing us to open and close them. It also helps us to lengthen the vocal folds to increase or decrease pitch. Imagine an elastic band. If you ping an elastic band and pull it tight, the pitch will increase. This is very similar to what the vocal folds do.

When you place your hand over your throat to locate the larynx, the main part you can feel is the THYROID CARTILAGE. This cartilage is the part that houses the vocal folds and is also known as the 'Adam's apple'.

Check out these diagrams of the larynx. Take a minute to familiarise yourself with all the parts and get used to how they sit together.

THE LARYNX
(FROM THE FRONT)

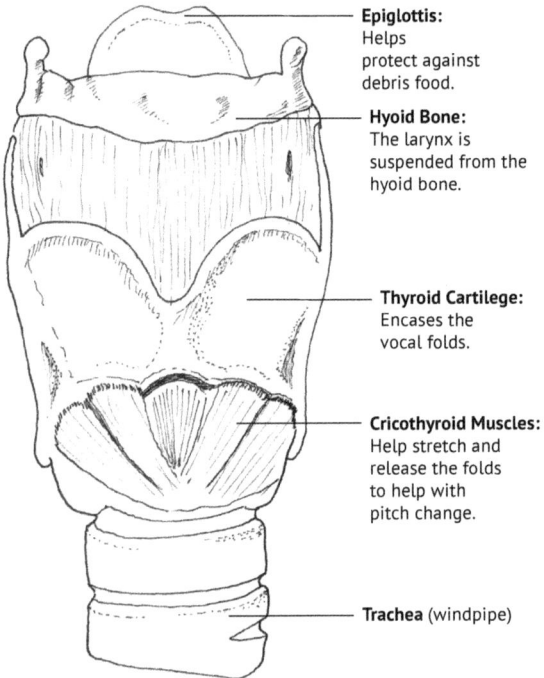

Epiglottis: Helps protect against debris food.

Hyoid Bone: The larynx is suspended from the hyoid bone.

Thyroid Cartilege: Encases the vocal folds.

Cricothyroid Muscles: Help stretch and release the folds to help with pitch change.

Trachea (windpipe)

You can't see the vocal folds on these diagrams, but you can see where they would sit, inside the thyroid cartilage.

THE LARYNX
(FROM THE BACK)

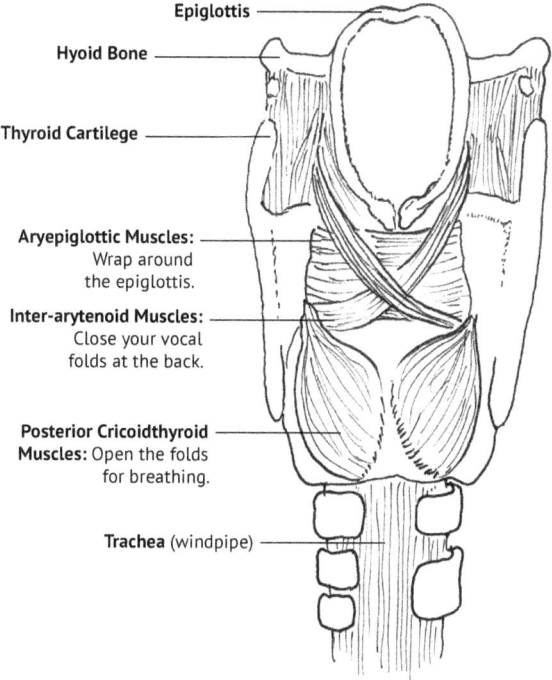

Epiglottis

Hyoid Bone

Thyroid Cartilege

Aryepiglottic Muscles:
Wrap around
the epiglottis.

Inter-arytenoid Muscles:
Close your vocal
folds at the back.

Posterior Cricoidthyroid
Muscles: Open the folds
for breathing.

Trachea (windpipe)

The Tract

It's important that you have an understanding of how the voice is laid out. Our vocal tract is the space that runs from just behind our nose to the top of our trachea (the windpipe). It includes the pharynx, the larynx, the mouth and tongue. Its primary function is a resonator, and the amazing thing is, we can change its shape and length. Let's have a go!

Elephant Burger:

Find a point on the side of your neck. Opening your mouth, simply flick the side of your neck. Remember to hold your breath while you do this. You should hear the sound changing. If it doesn't work the first time, move the position of the flick until you hear a hollow sound. This shows you that there is a lot of space in the vocal tract. Try shaping your mouth into vowel sounds 'OO' and 'EE'. Does it change the sound?. This shows you how your mouth and tongue position can really change the sound. This will come in very handy when you want to control your resonance later on. Take some time getting used to how your head, neck and mouth position can affect the sound you create.

⭐ Nugget!

So what is the pharynx? The PHARYNX is one of our main resonators. The top of the pharynx is positioned just behind the nasal cavity, this is called the NASOPHARYNX. It continues down behind our mouth (the OROPHARYNX) and ends just above the larynx (the LARYNGOPHARYNX). All this space is important when we are trying to create sound, and the sound needs space to resonate. The elephant burger you just did showed how you can change this resonating space to affect the sound you produce. The VOCAL TRACT is a term use to describe all the different components such as the larynx, the whole oral cavity and the pharynx.

The pharynx is only the space labelled on the diagram below. Remember: resonance is created by space.

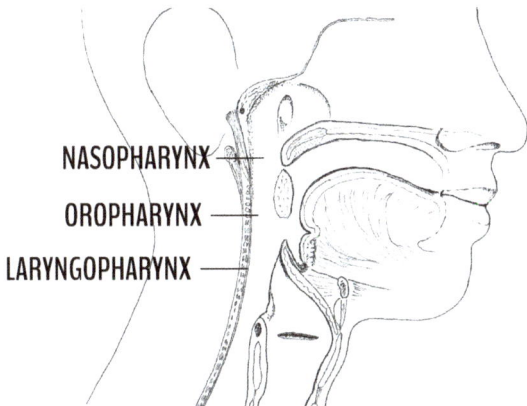

Let's Begin

I know we've already begun; this is something different. You've set up your breath and your posture, and you've begun to locate and use the voice. This elephant burger is all about how you start a sound. In the singing world, this is called 'onset' or 'attack' – I prefer to use the word onset as it feels a little less aggressive! There are different ways you can onset. We are going to focus on something called 'glottal onset'. You've actually already done it in a previous elephant burger (say what?!). Oh yes! Now it's time to bring attention to it and do it with purpose.

Elephant Burger:

The glottal onset is about bringing your vocal folds together before you make a sound. Simply say the words 'Uh, Oh' Where did this happen? It happened in your larynx. Before you make your 'Uh' sound, start to build up air behind the folds. This will give you a slight pushing sensation (remember those reasons the body has to push?). Make sure the movements are gentle; you don't need much pressure to locate the feeling. Once you've begun to build up pressure, let the vocal folds go to produce your 'Uh' sound. By controlling your vocal folds, you've managed to create a 'Glottal Onset'. (You're actually activating the arytenoid muscles to open and close the arytenoid cartilage and help move the vocal folds – see 'Larynx' – science!)

Now add in the whole sound 'Uh-oh'. Slow it down and notice when the glottal onset happens. When do you need to close your folds? You'll feel the same build-up of air behind the folds before you produce the 'uh' sound. Now proceed on to the 'Oh'. Notice this time how you have to close your folds again to produce the 'Oh' sound. You can isolate this feeling so you can move your vocal folds without even producing sound. You can simply open and close the vocal folds. Use the same process but don't build up the air this time. (You may notice a slight popping sensation in your larynx.) So when did you do this sound before? When you create most vowel sounds, it's easy to feel a glottal onset. A, E, I, O all use glottal onsets. When we sang the vowel 'AH' in our *Feel the Buzz* nugget you were probably using a glottal onset. Feel familiar?

This elephant burger was slightly more of an Elephant mixed grill, but hey! It's an interesting topic!

💪 Challenge!

Next time you find someone particularly interesting and want to agree with them, use the 'uh-huh' sound. They will think you are pleasantly agreeing with them but you will secretly know that you are practising your glottal onset. Sneaky...

⭐ Nugget!

So what are vocal folds? VOCAL FOLDS, also known as VOCAL CORDS are two flaps of membrane and muscle that come together to vibrate and create sound. They are between 12.5 and 23 mm in most adults and vibrate at roughly 110 cycles per second or Hz* for lower pitch (men),180–220 cycles per second for medium pitch (women) and 300 cycles per second for high registers (children). The vibrations increase as the pitch goes up and down.

You can imagine your vocal folds moving by placing the tip of your fingers and the heels of your hands together. Now create a wave movement starting at the heels of your hands and moving up to your fingers. This will give you an idea of how the folds vibrate. The heels of the hands show you the ends attached to the Arytenoid cartilage, which are pulled together and apart by the Arytenoid muscles. These come together to start the vibration of the folds. The Bernoulli's Principle does the rest!
(*see 'Hum Us a Tune'*).

One wave = 1 Hz or 1 'cycle'.

* Hz = 1 vibration per second and is the standard scientific unit of frequency.

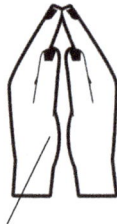

HEEL OF THE HAND

Interesting Fact: Our vocal folds are linked to our hormones. During a woman's cycle, the vocal folds can become tender making it harder to sing. The larynx and vocal folds also change shape and size as boys go through puberty.

Make Some Space

Today is all about space! We've met the larynx; now let's meet the vocal folds. We have two vocal folds that sit inside the thyroid cartilage. There are two sets of vocal folds: our true vocal folds (these are the ones that create sound) and our false vocal folds (this set is positioned above of our true vocal folds and protects them). However, the false vocal folds have no use to us when we want to create sound. If anything, they get in the way!

This elephant burger will help us move the false vocal folds out of the way so we have more space in the larynx.

Elephant Burger:

Locate your larynx to bring a little awareness to the exercise. Close your eyes and take some silent breaths. As you do this you should feel a sensation of space happening in your throat. If you connect this with your tummy-flop exercise, you'll notice how easy it is to let the air drop into your lungs! That's because we've got everything out of the way so the air can slide in and out easily.

Try this throughout the day and see if it changes anything about your speaking voice. If silent breathing doesn't work for you, try drinking an imaginary glass of water. Open your throat to allow the imaginary water to pour into your stomach.

⭐ Nugget!

But what is actually happening when we do a silent breath?

Let's try a few different positions to give you an idea of what is happening to your vocal folds. You're going to do three different positions. First, let's try a constricted position. Take a few breaths as if you are pretending to be a Dementor (remember those big scary things from Harry Potter?). It should be pretty hard to take a breath as your vocal folds are in the way! You'll notice that you are having to work harder with your abdominals to get the air to flow in and out.

Now relax your folds to make the Dementor sound a little quieter. Much easier, isn't it? But you can still hear something, can't you? That's because the air is still rushing past the vocal folds, which is creating a sound. Notice what has changed with your abdominals: they are more relaxed but there is still a little effort there. Now try your silent breath. This will deconstrict the false folds and move the true folds out of the way completely. Notice your abdominals. They are moving in and out very easily as there is nothing in the way of the air flow. Remember: this is just a breathing exercise. As you start to make sound, the vocal folds will start to close and open as you form vowels and consonants and change the pressure in your abdominals. Deconstricting the false vocal folds will set you up very nicely, though, and means that you don't add any unnecessary tension.

You can still keep this sensation of space as you start to voice sounds. If you feel tension start to creep in, simply stop and take a few silent breaths. Magic!

Hum Us a Tune

This section is all about HOW we make sound. We've spent some time finding out where the larynx is and what it feels like to make a sound. Now let's find out how we are making sound. Humming is a really great way to warm up the voice. It's safe and doesn't put any strain on the voice. You're going to go one step further and bring your tongue and your soft palate together. To do this, simply make an 'ng' sound.

Notice how the sound is now only travelling through your nose. If you pinch your nose the sound will stop completely! What fun!

Elephant Burger:

This elephant burger is nice and simple. You are going to hum a tune! Keep your tongue and your soft palate together and hum the tune of 'Ain't Nobody' by Chaka Khan.

Ain't Nobody

Rufus & Chaka Khan Arr: Ruth Royall

Ain't no - bo - dy   loves me   bet - ter

makes me   hap - py   makes me   feel   this___ way!

This melody only moves between a few notes, so it's very easy to follow. As you do the movement, notice what is happening to the back of your tongue. Is it lifting with the higher notes? If yes, that's totally normal! We have to lift our tongue a little to reach higher notes. If you feel any tension, do a couple of silent breaths to realign your larynx. Notice how much movement is happening in your abdominals and make sure you keep that tummy floppy on the in-breath!

Keep experimenting – you can do this exercise with any melody you choose. Just notice what is happening as you do it.

💪 Challenge!

Channel Chaka Khan and sing the chorus of 'Ain't Nobody' in front of the mirror with a hairbrush. Even better, do it with a friend!

⭐ Nugget!

So what is actually happening when we create sound?

Phonation! That's what!

PHONATION is the act of sending air from the lungs, up through the trachea (windpipe) and allowing it to hit our vocal folds, creating a vibration that produces sound. In order to produce sound, we need to make sure the vocal folds come together. Firm closure of the folds means we create a lovely, clear sound.

The back of the vocal folds are attached to the ARYTENOID CARTILAGES and the front to the THYROID CARTILAGE. When we breath in, the arytenoids open up, manoeuvring the vocal folds into an open position and allowing the air into our lungs (recognising this feeling will help with the tummy-flop exercise as it will be easier to feel the air 'drop in').

In order to create sound, we need to bring the vocal folds together so that they can start to oscillate.

The act of phonation uses something called 'Bernoulli's principle', which states that when air moves between two 'bodies', it creates an area of low pressure and this exerts a force which draws the two bodies closer together. Bernoulli demonstrated this by blowing air between two balloons and showing that they get closer together! Magic! Well, science, but you get the idea. Phonation works in exactly the same way but with the vocal folds instead of balloons.

Goalkeeper

You've spent a little time on your mechanism. This is all good stuff, but it's important not to forget about your body. The voice relies on our support and balance to function. As we know the voice works like a clock, each individual cog is important, so it's good to check in with ourselves and make sure everything is working as it should.

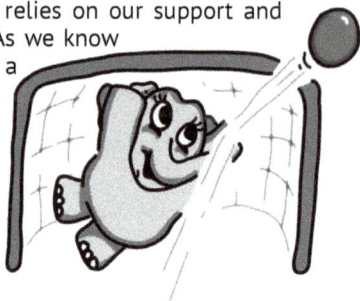

Elephant Burger:

This is all about posture. Imagine you are a goalkeeper. Keep your knees slightly bent and your arms out to the side as if you are ready to catch the ball. Notice how your spine aligns (you can also use your hips to help you align if you need to). Your body will stay flexible but ready. Try doing this while you wait for the bus, standing in line for your coffee or while you're waiting for your toast to pop.

Top Tip: *This exercise is also great on an exercise ball or balance trainer.*

Feeling Sleepy

But I'm just so tiiiiiired! Yawning is a great way to locate our soft palate. We use our soft palate to help shape sound.

Your soft palate is located at the roof of your mouth towards the top of your throat. If you place your thumb on the roof of your mouth, you will feel your hard palate. If you move your thumb towards the back, you should feel something squishy and soft; that is your soft palate.

Be careful not to push your finger too far back as you might make yourself heave! Blurgh! You can also use the tip of your tongue to feel it if you don't fancy giving it a poke!

Elephant Burger:

Let's start by getting the soft palate moving. Give a big yawn! You'll feel something lifting up; that's your soft palate! Now make an 'ng' sound. By making an 'ng' sound, you have brought your tongue and your soft palate together. This time, try making the same movement but without moving your mouth so you can feel the tongue and soft palate action at the back. Sounds easy but may take a few goes. Once you've got the hang of what's moving where, let's try some different sounds. Keeping your mouth and jaw loose, go between 'ng' and 'er'.

Remember: you don't need to use your jaw at all to create these sounds, only your tongue and soft palate. Notice how your tongue and soft palate come together to create the 'ng' and come apart when you make the 'er' sound. The 'er' sound is a much flatter shape – can you feel this in your tongue? See how important this is to help you create the different sounds.

⭐ Nugget!

The soft palate is a collection of muscle fibres and mucous membrane, and is responsible for closing off the nasal cavity when we swallow, thus protecting it from tiny bits of food. It can move up and down, and also be stretched sideways. When we create a rounded sound, such as 'oh', we lift our soft palate up. If we make a flat sound such as 'E' we flatten our soft palate out to the sides. Clever!

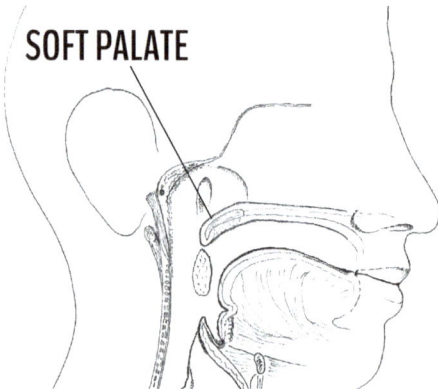

SOFT PALATE

Mini Movements

Singing is usually about subtle movements, so let's get the hang of this. We're going to use the soft palate to direct sound through our different resonance chambers.

Chambers? Resonance? What is this you speak of?! Remember we spoke about resonance waaaaaay back at the beginning? Well, it's time to start doing it! Like I said before, resonance is all about space. The shape of the space affects the shape of the sound.

Elephant Burger:

First, let me show you how the chambers work. Create an 'ng' sound. When you do this, you are sending the air through your nasal cavity. Now pinch your nose! Ha-ha! The noise stops completely. That's because the air is only travelling through your nose; when you pinch your nose, the sound has nowhere to go. You can actually seal off your nasal cavity completely so you are only using your mouth. This generally creates a brighter sound. Our mouth is a great resonating chamber. It's full of hard surfaces and it's nice and wet. Perfect! This is where our mini movements come in. Lift your soft palate up towards the yawn position (not all the way!) by making an 'ee' sound. As you make this sound, feel your soft palate lift up until you have sealed off the nasal cavity.

As you move your soft palate up, check to see if the air is still travelling through your nose by pinching it. If the sound changes, the air is still travelling through it. Keep going between 'ng' and 'ee' and feel the difference in movement. Notice how the sound is brighter on 'ee'. The nasal cavity is full of soft tissue that can sometimes deaden the sound of the voice. It is, however, very important to use the nasal cavity when pronouncing words such as 'sou-nn-d' or 'si-ng'. Notice how the soft palate and tongue move and you only use the nasal cavity in these sounds. Spend the day noticing the mini movements in your soft palate and tongue when you pronounce different words. Cool!

Bubbles!

You know that thing your mum always told you not to do? Well, it's great for the voice! Blowing bubbles through a straw can really help with 'vocal fold adduction'. What's that? Remember our nugget about phonation? ADDUCTION is a term we use to describe when the vocal folds come together. And remember how? That's right! 'Bernoulli's principle'. Blowing bubbles promotes healthy vocal fold closure and helps us either release tension or create better closure depending on the size of the straw.

Elephant Burger:

You can use this elephant burger as a warm-up and a warm-down. Let's start by using a larger straw or tube. A bit of rubber tubing from a hardware store about 10–13 mm wide is perfect! Using a larger straw will relieve any muscle tension you may have, so it's perfect for a tired voice. Find a bottle and fill it with about five centimetres of water. Submerge the tube about two centimetres beneath the water and blow into the tube to create bubbles. Keep the breaths consistent. Now try singing down the straw; keep it underneath the water as you sing. You only need to do this for a minute or two. You can do it first thing in the morning as part of your morning stretch or in the evening after a long day at work. If you are about to sing a song then I definitely recommend doing this before and after. Just blowing through a straw for a couple of minutes a day can help improve tone and quality and even increase your range!

⭐ Nugget!

So what is this straw thing all about? Well, it's all about physics. You know about the Bernoulli principle. It's the same thing that keeps planes in the air and makes a flag flutter in the wind. By using straw phonation (the act of humming or 'vocalising' through a straw), we are helping to increase air flow in the vocal tract, which in turn promotes a healthy oscillation (opens and closes) of the vocal folds. The straw also promotes something called 'back pressure'. Back pressure is when the acoustic pressure that starts at the level of the vocal folds is sent up through the vocal tract and bounces off the lips. This is then reflected back down towards the vocal folds to help them vibrate with more ease and less muscular effort. Neat!

💪 Challenge!

Make yourself a bubble blower. Get a bottle with a lid and a straw or some rubber tubing from the hardware store. Cut a hole in the lid the size of the tube and secure it in place with some sticky tape. Decorate your bottle with whatever takes your fancy and voilà! You have yourself a rather fancy bubble blower. If you find you have a little tension in your singing practice, go for a bigger tube. If you find you are a little breathy then try a straw. If you're not sure, it's always good to see a vocal coach. They will be able to tell you what you need and what works well with your voice.

Speaking in Pitch

Even if you struggle with pitch, we all have a natural place that our voice sits. Working out where this is will really help you work out what range you are. It's as easy as...

1, 2, 3!

Elephant Burger:

If you have a piano then great! If not, there are loads of free apps with a keyboard. Speak the words 'one, two, three'. Just use your normal speaking voice. See if you can work out where on the keyboard your voice is sitting. If you have a female voice, the likelihood is it will be somewhere in the upper middle. If you have a male voice, it will be lower down. If you have a very young voice, it will be further up. Remember that everyone is different and one size doesn't fit all. I have a fairly low female voice, for instance, and my speaking voice can sometimes match some male voices. This is just to give you a ballpark figure of what to expect. Keep speaking the words 'one, two, three' until you find roughly three notes that the words match.

Now try raising the pitch by two notes. This may make your three words sound a little more surprised or alert. Now try dropping the pitch by two notes (below where your voice sits naturally). This may make you sound a little more earnest. Spend the day noticing what happens to the pitch of your voice as you are speaking. Notice how the pitch lifts and drops as you speak and as you say different things with different inflections.

💪 **Challenge!**

Have a conversation with a friend two notches up from where you would normally speak and see if they notice. Only two notches won't strain or push your voice, but it may make you sound a little brighter!

Top Tip: Remember to keep using your body and breath elephant burgers! It's sometimes easy to forget when we get into the science-y bits!

Jaws

Cue the theme! OK, so this elephant burger isn't about a giant man-eating shark, it's about our jaw. Jaw tension is something you want to avoid if you can. Remember how I said how big the tongue is? Well, the jaw is pretty big too. The muscles that close it are used for chewing and are some of the strongest muscles in the body. This means it can often hold a lot of tension. We're going to try and keep it nice and slack.

Elephant Burger:

This is about creating something called 'slack jaw'. When we bite down hard, we are using a muscle called the MASSETER MUSCLE. Remember that all the muscles in the body pull? Well, this muscle pulls the jaw up towards our head. Start by tensing your jaw and pulling this muscle up, then simply let it go and hang loose. Try doing this in front of a mirror both with your lips open and closed. You probably won't actually notice that much change in the look of your face. It often feels a lot more than it looks. Now try making a sound while keeping your jaw slack. You are going to create a slow 'B' sound. Let the air pressure build up behind your lips and then gently let it go, creating a soft 'buh' sound. Notice what happens to your jaw. Does it stay loose? This is a great exercise to help release jaw tension.

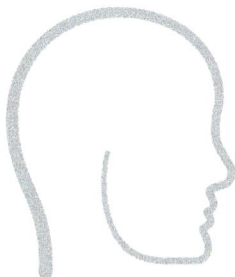

Registers

Disclaimer – Registers often spark a bit of confusion with the terminology that is used. It really doesn't matter what terminology you use as long as you understand how it feels. You may have heard the terms 'head' and 'chest' voice or 'modal' and 'falsetto'. They both mean the same thing.

'Chest' and 'modal' refer to our speaking voice, which has a heavier, thicker quality and 'head' and 'falsetto' refer to our thinner, lighter voice quality. I'm going to use the terms modal and falsetto just so we all know where we stand.

Elephant Burger:

Let's start with our modal register. Speak the words 'oh yeah' then slow it right down to 'ooooohh yeeeaaaah'. Notice the quality of this sound. It's fuller, maybe louder. Make sure you are speaking this sound. Now let's pitch this sound. Find your speaking pitch and speak the words over a single note 'ooooohh yeeeaaaah'. Now try over two notes – 'oh' over one and 'yeah' over the other. Keep paying attention to the quality of your voice. Does it still have that spoken quality? Well done. That is modal! Now let's try finding falsetto. Imagine your friend is standing on the other side of the road and you need to get their attention. 'Yoo-hoo!' Let the sound lift and soar. You should notice a different quality when you do this: a higher, thinner quality. Make sure you aren't lifting your modal register and shouting.

The sound should have a Micky Mouse quality to it. Try this a few times until it feels soft and easy. Well done. This is falsetto!

⭐ Nugget!

The vocal folds are made up of three layers. The inner layer is called the MUSCULUS VOCALIS layer and is the thickest part of the fold. The middle layer is the LIGAMENT and the outer layer is the MUCOSA, which is a very thin mucus tissue. When we are in modal, most used for the speaking voice, the muscular layer (MUSCULUS VOCALIS) is engaged and moving and creates a vibration through all of the layers. This creates a much thicker, richer sound. When we are in falsetto, only the outer layer of the vocal fold, the MUCOSA is oscillating, and the muscular layer is relaxed, creating a much thinner and seemingly higher quality. Falsetto often has a much higher range but doesn't necessarily mean that we have to sing high. We can still take this register fairly low down.

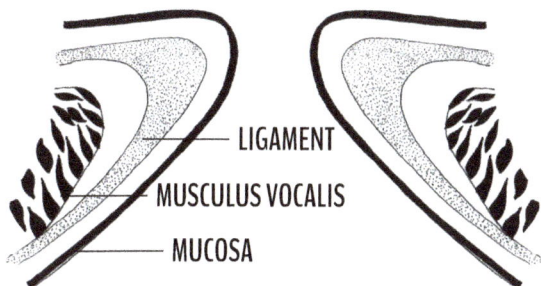

LIGAMENT
MUSCULUS VOCALIS
MUCOSA

Let's Have a Whinge

There are all sorts of different ways you can use your modal register. We don't just have one setting; there are lots! Whinging helps us lift our modal register up without shouting or straining. Magic!

Elephant Burger:

Imagine someone has just stolen your favourite toy, you know, the really good one! Make a small whinge – 'oooowww' – and let the sound slide up. Try to stay in your modal register and not slip into falsetto. Notice what happens as you do this and adjust any tension you may feel. You may need to deconstrict the false folds by taking a few silent breaths or give the tongue a little stretch. All this is good practice! Try a few different whinge phrases; 'oohh noo' is a good one. Now try counting with this same whinge quality. Lengthen out the numbers so you really feel the whinge quality and stay high up in your range. Now try pitching the numbers with the same quality. Well done! This is high modal and what a lot of contemporary singers use.

⭐ Nugget!

So how does our voice do this? Well, it's all about the layers. Remember how I said our muscular layer is engaged when we are in modal register? We can engage it to different levels to make it more flexible. When we use a thick speaking quality to our voice, our muscular layer is fully engaged. When we create a high whinge quality, our muscular layer is only partly engaged, creating a more flexible vocal fold, which can go higher. We are still using our muscular layer; we are just not engaging every part of it, meaning we create a different quality and a higher range. Whoa!!

Mickey Mouse

Character voices are a really great way to help you master your technique. By impersonating something we already know the sound of, our body instinctively puts all the correct things in all the correct places to create this sound. Clever! We're going to be working on our falsetto register in this elephant burger.

Elephant Burger:

'Hello, Pluto!' Remember Micky Mouse and his distinctive voice? Try giving it a go! Notice what is happening to your voice. You've switched into that higher, thinner quality. Now lengthen the sound out. 'Heeeeyy, Pluuuuuuto!' Keep that same quality in your voice and notice how it affects the air flow. Higher notes don't need as much breath. Notice how the effort level in your abdominals has dropped slightly from your usual speaking voice. Try some different sounds – 'yoo-hoooo' is a good one and 'weeeeeeee'. Keep having fun noticing when your voice transitions into falsetto throughout the day (it will probably be more often than you think!).

⭐ Nugget!

So what happens when we take a note higher? Remember our nugget about layers? When we make a sound in our falsetto, only the outer layer of the vocal fold is vibrating (the mucosa). This is what changes the quality of our voice. When we produce a pitched note, our vocal folds are vibrating at a particular frequency. They vibrate faster to produce higher notes and slower to produce lower notes. In order to produce a higher note, the vocal fold needs to stretch and lengthen to produce that higher pitch. Imagine an elastic band. When we ping it, it makes a sound; if we stretch it that sound becomes higher. This is the same as what happens to our vocal folds. But how? Remember our thyroid cartilage? The vocal folds are attached at one end to the inside of the thyroid cartilage and to the arytenoids at the other.

When we engage the cricothyroid muscle, the thyroid cartilage can tip forward, stretching the vocal folds. This means they vibrate faster, just like our elastic band (whaaaat!). We can also tip our cricoid cartilage backwards, which has the same effect. People tend to do one or the other. It doesn't matter which one your body does, they both have the same result! So when we lift a note higher, this is what's happening inside our larynx. We can do this whether we're in modal or falsetto. Pretty awesome!

Turn Up The Volume!

There are a few ways you can increase volume in your voice without putting in lots of effort. It's all about position. It's important to make sure you have enough air flow and ensure you are supporting your voice properly with your posture and balance. You've already explored whinging. Lifting your modal up will naturally make your voice sound a little louder (higher notes are louder, that's just physics!), but how do we project any note? Resonance! By using resonance, we can safely project our voice without causing any strain or discomfort.

Elephant Burger:

By reducing the space at the back of your mouth, you are able to increase the volume easily. Think of it like this: imagine a hose pipe where the water is spraying all over the place, if you adjust the nozzle to a smaller setting you will create a jet of water. A similar theory relates to the voice; by creating a smaller space, we are creating a jet of sound as the sound has plenty to bounce off (remember how resonance works). By doing this, we also reduce the amount of air we need to produce the note, so we are far less likely to run out of air quickly. You are going to work with an 'ee' tongue position. Check out the diagram and familiarise yourself with the different positions. Let's have a look at the vowel sounds so you know exactly what sound you're making. Try making these sounds with just your tongue and not your lips and jaw!

- 'ee' as in sheep
- 'er' as in bird
- 'eh' as in bed
- 'ah' as in far

Work with the 'ee' position on the diagram. You'll feel your tongue lifting at the back. Now lengthen that sound out to 'nee-y-aa'. How does your tongue move? The tip will lift to create the 'n', then lift at the back, then drop down.

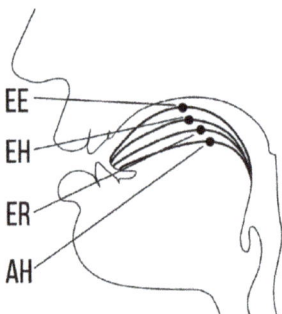

EE

EH

ER

AH

Focus on keeping that small space at the back of your mouth for the whole sound. Does it increase the volume? Remember: these movements are small.

Now try mixing the 'ee' and 'eh' position with your whinge sound. You can even progress to 'nah nah nah nah naaa naaa' (imagine you are sticking your tongue out in a playground like a naughty kid!). This produces quite a twangy sound.

The voice is subtle and you don't have to produce such extreme sounds to be able to increase the volume with your vowel sounds. See if you can colour words with this 'l' shape.

You'll notice that your tongue wants to move between 'ee', 'eh' and 'uh'. Let it do its thing but focus on the lifted positions at the back. Make 'ee' your default so all the sounds are coloured with the twangy resonance. You'll be able to feel that you don't need as much breath when using these positions, as the sounds you are producing are naturally much louder.

Spend the day working with these tongue positions and notice how your voice cranks up to 11!

Shape The Sound

This bit is so fun! You've learnt how to control your breath and balance your posture, You're starting to understand how your vocal mechanism works and how your vocal folds behave.

Now is the part where you get to shape the sound!

Resonance is about space: when the space changes, the tone of the sound changes, and we can do this with our tongue.

You've already become somewhat acquainted with your soft palate; now let's feel what happens when you navigate those vowels.

Elephant Burger:

We're going to move between the sound 'ah' and 'ee'. 'Ah' is a round sound and 'ee' is a flat sound. Remember to focus on your tongue when you do this (*see 'Feeling Sleepy'*). Notice how the tongue moves between these sounds to create the different vowel. Now let's try colouring a whole line with the same vowel. Let's sing the first line of 'Hey Jude'.

As you go through the words, keep your tongue in a lower 'ah' position. Notice how it darkens the sound. Bear in mind your tongue will move to create the different vowels and consonants; our aim is to give an overall colour to the sound. Now try it with an 'ee' vowel: your tongue will lift at the back to create this sound. Notice how the sound becomes a little brighter. There are many different subtleties to these resonances and you may experience more than just these two sounds.

Hey Jude

The Beatles Arr: Ruth Royall

This is the beauty of the voice; it's full of nuance! Experiment with the different vowel shapes and how you can colour sounds by changing the position of your tongue. It's so much fun!

I hope you've enjoyed this *Pocket Guide to The Voice*. You should have a fairly clear understanding of the different elements to the voice now and how to navigate them. This book can be used as many times as you like. All the elephant burgers are meant to be incorporated in your regular singing practice for a healthy voice. Remember to warm up and warm down and most of all enjoy yourself!

If you feel you want to take your practice further then you can! I've listed some of the books I read on my own vocal journey, and I highly recommend you taking a read as well! You can also find me at www.ruthroyall.com and keep up to date with other projects and products I've got coming out.

Keep up the good work!

Bye for now from
Ellie and me.

Further Reading...

If this has sparked your thirst for knowledge then read on...

This book was an absolute pleasure to write, and it was an even greater pleasure doing the research.

Here are some of the books I used as research and would highly recommend.

This is a Voice
– Gillyanne Kayes & Jeremy Fisher

The Power of Habit: Why We Do What We Do, And How To Change – Charles Duhigg

So You Want To Sing Gospel
– Trineice Robinson-Martin

Singing and the Actor
– Gillyanne Kayes

If in Doubt, Breathe Out!
– Ron Morris & Linda Hutchison

Stay Connected...

It's been great working with you! If you'd like to get in touch then you can!

facebook/ruthroyallmusic

instagram/ruthroyallvocals

www.ruthroyall.com

I'd love to hear your thoughts about this book and what it did for you!

www.ingramcontent.com/pod-product-compliance
Lightning Source LLC
Chambersburg PA
CBHW042339040426
42448CB00019B/3341